A Polar Bear's World

Katie Gillespie

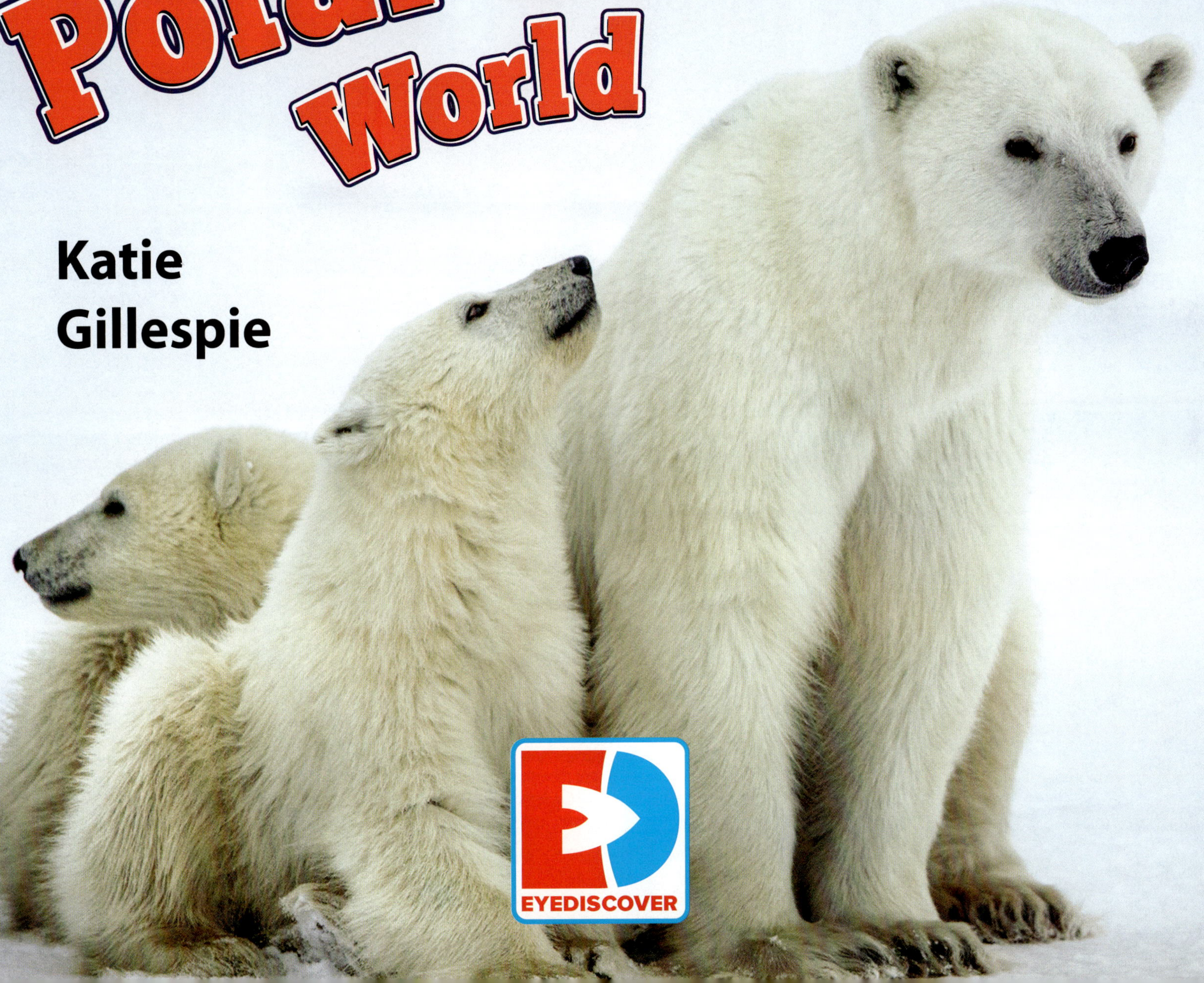

EYEDISCOVER

Go to **www.eyediscover.com** and enter this book's unique code.

BOOK CODE

U529555

EYEDISCOVER brings you optic readalongs that support active learning.

Published by AV² by Weigl
350 5th Avenue, 59th Floor New York, NY 10118
Website: www.eyediscover.com

Library of Congress Control Number: 2017930723

ISBN 978-1-4896-5680-3 (hardcover)

Printed in the United States of America
in Brainerd, Minnesota
1 2 3 4 5 6 7 8 9 0 21 20 19 18 17

022017
020317

Editor: Katie Gillespie
Designer: Mandy Christiansen

Weigl acknowledges Getty Images, iStock, and Shutterstock as the primary image suppliers for this title.

EYEDISCOVER provides enriched content, optimized for tablet use, that supplements and complements this book. EYEDISCOVER books strive to create inspired learning and engage young minds in a total learning experience.

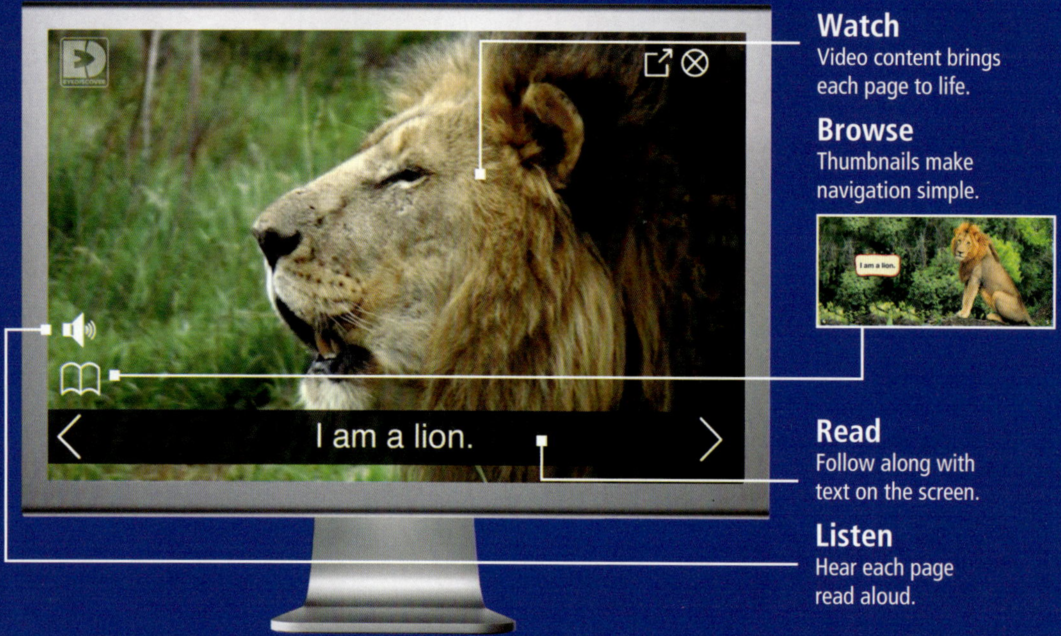

Your EYEDISCOVER Optic Readalongs come alive with...

Audio
Listen to the entire book read aloud.

Video
High resolution videos turn each spread into an optic readalong.

OPTIMIZED FOR

- ✓ TABLETS
- ✓ WHITEBOARDS
- ✓ COMPUTERS
- ✓ AND MUCH MORE!

A Polar Bear's World

In this book, you will learn about

- how I look
- where I live
- what I eat

and much more!

I am a polar bear.

I have white fur and a black nose. I am one of the biggest bears on Earth.

I live in the Arctic
where it is very cold.

My large paws work like snowshoes. They keep me from falling on the ice.

I had no teeth when I was born. I could not see until I was about one month old.

I am a meat eater.
Seals are my favorite food.

I am a very good hunter. I can smell my food from far away.

I love to go swimming.
I spend more time under
water than any other bear.

I need large patches of ice where I can hunt in order to stay healthy.

POLAR BEARS BY THE NUMBERS

The **heaviest** polar bear ever found weighed **2,209 pounds**. That is about as much as **some small cars.** (803 kilograms)

Polar bears can **live** for up to **30 years** in nature.

A polar bear can **hold its breath under water** for more than **one minute.**

A **newborn** polar bear cub weighs only 1 pound at birth. (0.45 kg) This is about the **size** of a **kitten**.

There are between **20,000 and 25,000** polar bears left **in the Arctic**.

Each of a polar bear's **five toes** has a **curved claw**.

KEY WORDS

Research has shown that as much as 65 percent of all written material published in English is made up of 300 words. These 300 words cannot be taught using pictures or learned by sounding them out. They must be recognized by sight. This book contains 51 common sight words to help young readers improve their reading fluency and comprehension. This book also teaches young readers several important content words, such as proper nouns. These words are paired with pictures to aid in learning and improve understanding.

Page	Sight Words First Appearance
4	a, am, I
7	and, Earth, have, of, on, one, the, white
8	in, is, it, live, very, where
11	from, keep, large, like, me, my, they, work
12	about, could, had, no, not, old, see, until, was, when
15	are, food
16	away, can, far, good
19	any, go, more, other, than, time, to, under, water
20	need

Page	Content Words First Appearance
4	polar bear
7	fur, nose
8	Arctic
11	ice, paws, snowshoes
12	month, teeth
15	meat eater, seals
16	hunter
20	patches

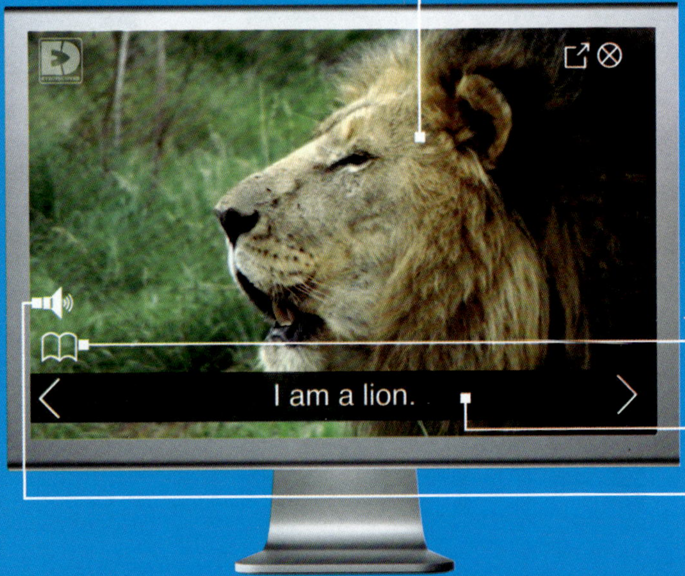

Watch
Video content brings each page to life.

Browse
Thumbnails make navigation simple.

Read
Follow along with text on the screen.

Listen
Hear each page read aloud.

EYEDISCOVER

Go to www.eyediscover.com and enter this book's unique code.

BOOK CODE

U529555